AUTHORITY
FACEBOOK
Live

How To Use Facebook Live To Engage
With Your Audience, Build Your Brand
And Sell More of Your Products

Disclaimer

This book has been written for information purposes only. Every effort has been made to make this book as complete and accurate as possible. However, there may be mistakes in typography or content. Also, this book provides information only up to the publishing date. Therefore, this book should be used as a guide - not as the ultimate source.

The purpose of this book is to educate. The author and the publisher does not warrant that the information contained in this book is fully complete and shall not be responsible for any errors or omissions. The author and publisher shall have neither liability nor responsibility to any person or entity with respect to any loss or damage caused or alleged to be caused directly or indirectly by this book.

FACEBOOK LIVE AUTHORITY

About the Author

Bill Price is an entrepreneur living in the US who loves sharing knowledge and helping others on the topic of Social Media and Digital Marketing

Bill is a passionate person who will go the extra mile and over-deliver.

Bill's words of wisdom:

"I believe that knowledge is power. Everyone should improve themselves and/or business, no matter what stage in life they're in. Whether it's to develop a better mindset or to increase profits. Moving forward is key."

If you would like to learn more from Bill Price, please visit:

www.businessbeginshere.com

FACEBOOK LIVE AUTHORITY

Table of Contents

Introduction

Live streaming is poised to become very much the next 'big thing'. This is an entirely new way to create content that allows us to communicate directly with an audience in a highly engaging manner. It's new, it's exciting and it's still growing rapidly at this point.

As a digital marketer, this should all make you very excited. A large part of our job is to be able to spot emerging digital trends and to get there before anyone else. When we do this well, it enables us to capture an audience before the competition and potentially to find more effective ways to influence our customers and build our relationship.

This is exactly what live streaming represents for the savvy and it's exactly the reason that big players like Tai Lopez are investing such a lot of time into services like Meerkat. Right now, almost anyone can create a live stream about anything and come away with new followers on Meerkat or Periscope. This simply reflects the fact that those platforms are *so* exciting and that there is still so little competition there.

But if you *really* want evidence that live streaming is about to take off in a big way, you only need to look to Facebook Live for evidence. No doubt Facebook is one of the leaders in this industry, so the fact that it has introduced its own version of a live streaming service is pretty much as sure sign that it's on the up and up.

Of course the fact that Facebook is entering this space is also somewhat *bad* news for the other players like Meerkat and Periscope. And it also changes the game somewhat for the rest of us. While Periscope is owned by Twitter, Facebook is still likely to be able to put a lot more clout into live streaming now and this will only be increased by the much tighter integration that live has with the Facebook platform.

In this book we're going to learn in a lot more detail what makes live streaming so exciting and why it's even *more* exciting that Facebook is involved. What's more, you'll see exactly how to get started with your own Facebook Live videos and how to begin building a big audience and interacting with that audience in a far more engaged and effective manner...

Stats and Figures

Not sure if live streaming is really all it's cracked up to be? Then check out some of these impressive statistics that will pretty much nip any doubts you may have in the bud...

Did you know for example, that Periscope already has well over 10,000,000 user accounts? And if you were to combine all the footage that has ever been recorded through the platform, it would take over 40 years to watch all of it! Of those 10 million accounts, 2 million are active every single day – across 25 different countries.

On the day that Periscope launched, it got a whopping 60k Tweets! Twitter went on to buy

Periscope for $100 million – another very impressive vote of confidence for the platform!

Meanwhile, Meerkat has also done incredibly well. This live streaming service launched around the same time as Periscope with 120,000 users signed up by the end of just the first month. And these aren't the only services that have been doing exceedingly well either!

Twitch for example is a streaming service for gaming specifically and had as many as 12 billion users at the end of 2014! Another is Blab – a streaming app which shows a lot of promise and has the unique feature of allowing multiple people to stream at once in a conference-type setting. This platform demonstrates excellent engagement, with people spending 65 minutes a day watching video on average!

YouTube has also been getting involved. The company now streams events and lets users create their own live content. In 2015, the company streamed the gaming expo 'E3' and that video was viewed by over 8 *million* viewers in just 12 hours!

All the data and all the stats point to the inescapable truth that live streaming is very likely to be a *big* deal for the future of the web.

What You Will Learn in This Book

In this book, we're going to learn all about live streaming in general and live streaming on Facebook *in particular*. You'll learn everything that you could possibly need to know in order to start taking full advantage of this incredible opportunity and this amazing platform for a whole new type of content.

Specifically, you will learn:

- The history of live streaming
- What makes live streaming so unique
- What your options are when it comes to creating live content
- Why Facebook is getting involved and why this is big news for marketers
- How to get set up with your own Facebook Live account
- How to build a Facebook page and grow your audience

- How to create live content for Facebook
- Tips to make your live videos as engaging and exciting as possible
- Strategies for monetizing and utilizing live streaming
- Instructions on how to use advanced features of the platform
- The future of live streaming and Facebook Live
- And much more!

Chapter 1: The History of Facebook and Live Streaming

As mentioned in the introduction, live streaming is *very* big news for the web and is something that many speculators are watching very closely right now. But where did live streaming come from? What precisely is it? And why is Facebook getting involved?

Before we dive into the nitty gritty and discuss how to get started and how to create content, let's rewind a little and go over some of the history of live streaming and of Facebook so that you can get to grips with the lay of the land...

What is Live Streaming and Why it Matters?

As the name suggests, 'live streaming' means that you're filming videos and streaming them live. So instead of creating content using a camera, editing it and then uploading it to YouTube, you are instead filming and streaming directly. This is raw footage, broadcast live and it's incredibly exciting.

Normally, live streaming will take place via an app. To do this, you simply need to install the specific app on your smartphone (which will normally be either Meerkat or Periscope) and then you'll hit the stream button. You may also set up some details about the nature of the video – giving it a name, a picture and/or a simple description.

From there, you then record with the camera in your phone and anyone can watch from around the world who is signed in, or who sees you Tweet that you're going live. There are also plugins for your website (if you use WordPress) that allow people to see if you're live and then tune in to watch if they so desire.

So what is it about this type of content that makes it so unique and so effective?

Well many people have described it as the closest thing to teleporting. If you load up Periscope for instance, then you can view a map showing where all the feeds are coming from and then simply select which one you would like to view. This is quite a surreal experience, as you will then be transported into a person's room, or even to a concert. You can now see the world through their eyes, *as* it is happening. Imagine being able to watch concerts live, comedy acts or parties that you were unable to attend!

And imagine how this could impact world events once this form of content really takes off! Imagine if there was a tsunami or a hurricane and if you could then view the events unfold from multiple points of view all around the world all at once. It would almost be like being omnipresent during that event!

For marketers this is also huge. There is something that viewers find remarkably exciting about watching something live and this also gives them the ability to ask questions, have discussion and get feedback live.

Imagine reviewing a product that you created during a live feed. You could build a huge audience and at the same time answer questions that show up and even show off other aspects of the product that you might otherwise have glossed over.

Many marketers are also doing regular live streams: having live discussions with their viewers over their morning cup of coffee. This allows an unprecedented level of intimacy that can help you to build a much closer relationship with your audience and create much more engagement.

These are the reasons that people are excited about live content online – and there are many other potential applications and uses for this type of content. Imagine being able to view a restaurant live, right in that moment before you book a table. Or imagine being able to see behind the scenes while your favorite TV show is being filmed.

The History of Live Streaming So Far

Before Facebook's involvement, most people thought of Periscope as being the major player in the live streaming stakes. Actually though, it was

Meerkat that was the very first to market and that really kicked things off. And back then, no one had heard of Periscope, which make Meerkat definitely a very exciting piece of news for pundits.

Meerkat was drawing a lot of attention very quickly then when it was first announced in March 2015. From then, it managed to create an increasing amount of buzz and gather a flurry of media attention. Ironically, Meerkat also worked very closely alongside Twitter, which really helped to give it a boost. Back then, Meerkat was known as 'AIR' and later on 'Yevvo'.

But soon Twitter would decide that simply supporting Meerkat wasn't enough. The hype surrounding live streaming was clear and so the company needed its own offering. Thus they bought the smaller and much lesser known Periscope for a nice sum of $100 million. Very quickly, Periscope rose to prominence with Twitter behind it.

Periscope very quickly proved that there is a huge audience and massive potential for this type of content and that's no doubt what piqued the interest of Facebook – the 'other' massive social media network.

The History of Facebook so Far

That's the history of live streaming up to the point of Facebook's involvement. But how about the history of Facebook itself?

Most people know a little about the history of Facebook thanks to the successful movie *The Social Network*. Despite being a good film though, many of the facts presented are inaccurate and the story is only loosely based on the real events.

As shown in the film, Facebook was the brain child of Mark Zuckerberg who was studying at Harvard at the time. Also as shown in the film, Mark had previously experienced some success and controversy after creating 'Face Mash'.

In the film, Mark is shown as being socially awkward and as using Facebook as a means to try and enter college clubs and attract women. In fact though, Mark was already dating his now-wife Priscilla Chan at the time he came up with the social network! Also somewhat accurate is the depiction of Mark's partnership with roommate and colleague Eduardo Saverin. It's also true that Mark faced legal charges from the Winklevoss twins and their friend Divya Narenda.

However, it's also very unlikely that Mark really took inspiration from the trio when creating Facebook. In fact, it was public knowledge at the time that Harvard was working on their own social network but that they were taking a long time to complete the project. Mark discussed this openly with the *Harvard Crimson* and it appears more likely that this was the competition he was more focussed on:

"It is clear that the technology needed to create a centralized Website is readily available … the benefits are many.

"Everyone's been talking a lot about a universal face book within Harvard. I think it's kind of silly that it would take the University a couple of years to get around to it as I can do it better than they can, and I can do it in a week."

After creating 'The Facebook' in blue (owing to Mark's color-blindness) he put it on the Kirkland House online mailing list, which had 300 subscribers.

By the end of the first night, the site already had between 1,200-1,500 new members.

Initially, Facebook was only available to Harvard students but gradually it would be rolled out across other colleges and then eventually certain businesses and schools before being opened to the public. This gradually roll-out really helped the site to pick up steam in those early days. In 2004, Facebook expanded to include Stanford, Columbia and Yale and from there it continued to grow.

Over the years that followed, Facebook would go on to add many new additional features that today are considered a core part of the platform. For instance, it wasn't until 2006 that the company introduced its 'News Feed' that initially received some backlash.

And it wasn't until 2010 that we saw the introduction of a 'Like' button. This was also the year that Facebook Messages were introduced.

Today, Facebook has more active users than the population of any given country in the world. In fact, as of September 2015, 1.01 billion people were logging into the site daily. There are over 1.39 billion users on Facebook mobile alone, while the like and share buttons get over 10 million views a day on other websites. There are over 300 million photographs uploaded every single day and the average American will spend 40 minutes a day on the site!

But the impact of Facebook can't even be accurately captured by these admittedly impressive numbers. Facebook has become much more than just a social network and today can be considered an integral part of modern life. Many terms such as 'friend me' and 'like' have been added to the global lexicon and Facebook has even arguably had an impact on the way we socialize and on our psychology more broadly. This isn't just a tool – it's something that is fundamentally changing human interaction.

Acquisitions, Development and Live Streaming

It's in this context that we need to view Facebook's interest in live streaming and its move into this area. For a tool that has genuinely altered the way we communicate and the way we stay in touch, live streaming makes all the sense in the world.

Facebook allows us to share our experiences with people around the world by uploading photos and writing comments. But now it is going a step further than that by letting us share those moments and memories *live* with people.

And considering the billions of daily users, there is no company in the world that is quite as well poised to really corner this market. Periscope and Meerkat are no doubt concerned!

Chapter 2: Facebook Live – What You Need to Know to Get Started

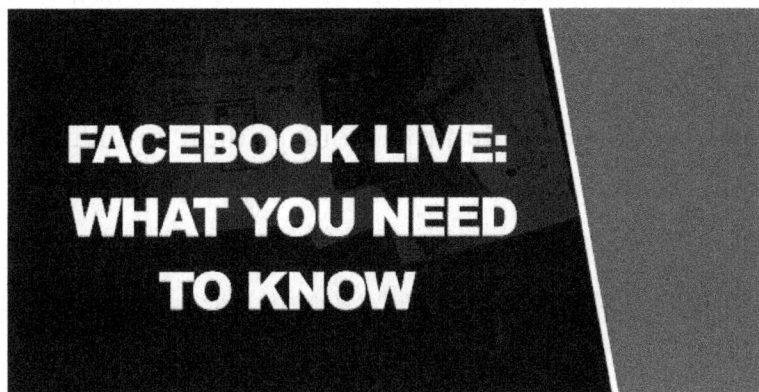

At this point in the story you know the state of Facebook and you know the state of live video. Now it's time to see how the two collided. And once you've been introduced to Facebook Live, you can learn the basics to get started!

Facebook Live was actually introduced in December 2015. And right away, Facebook really made a big push for it. March 1st, 2016 really demonstrates this:

"We rolled out Facebook Live on iOS in December and last week we began rolling it out on Android in the US. Over the last three months Facebook Live video has become more and more popular and more and more people and Pages are creating and watching live videos."

The company stated that people watch Facebook Live videos three times as much as other video content on the site. In response, the company adjusted the algorithm to encourage more visibility for this kind of content.

"Now that more and more people are watching Live videos, we are considering Live Videos as a new content type – different from normal videos – and learning how to rank them for people in News Feed. As a first step, we are making a small update to News Feed so that Facebook Live videos are more likely to appear higher in News Feed when those videos are actually live, compared to after they are no longer live. People spend more than 3x more time watching a Facebook Live video on average compared to a video that's no longer live. This is because Facebook Live videos are more interesting in the moment than after the fact."

Facebook also states that users are actually more *engaged* with live content – and that viewers are ten times more likely to leave a comment on a live video versus one that is not live.

This is all a clear sign that Facebook has been invested in live from the start and now the feature has been rolled out to include people all around the world (Facebook Live was initially only available in the US). They also introduced some new interesting features – such as 'reactions' and the ability to post live content inside of groups (more on this later!). The company is also discussing introducing filters, similar to those found in Instagram. The 'Facebook Live Map' is also another sign that Facebook is invested in this technology.

Mark even went on to tell *Buzzfeed News* that he 'wouldn't be surprised if you fast-forward five years and most of the content that people see on Facebook and are sharing on a day-to-day basis is video'.

This also works in tandem with other features like 'Sports Stadium' for aggregated sports commentary – which aims to provide live feedback and coverage on sports as you're watching them. The company has even shown interest in livestreaming sporting events for its users!

How to Use Facebook Live

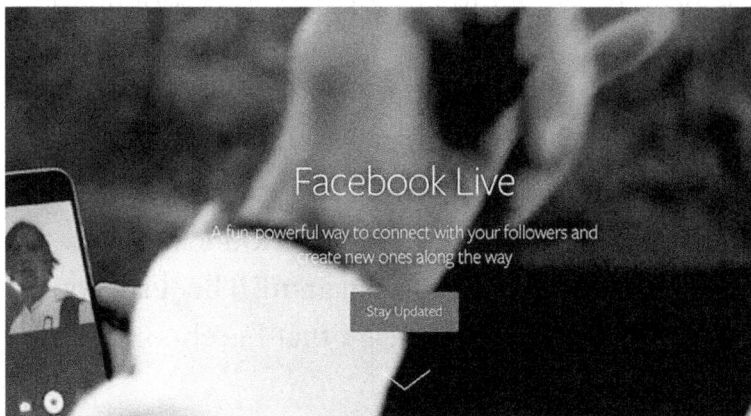

Despite all this hype, excitement and focus though, it actually wouldn't have been all that hard to miss the introduction of Live. The feature just kind of subtly 'appeared' on the app and there wasn't all that much fanfare surrounding it from a user's perspective. Thus you may well be completely unaware as to how you would go about creating a live video!

The first thing to recognize then is that this is a tool that you use with the Facebook app and not something you can do through the website. This is in keeping with other types of live streaming apps like Periscope and Meerkat.

1. Tell fans when you're broadcasting ahead of time.

Build anticipation by letting your audience know when you'll be going live with a written post. We've found one day's notice gives people the right amount of time to tune in.

2. Go live when you have a strong connection.

Check the app to make sure that you have a strong signal before going live. WiFi tends to work best, but if you can't find a nearby network, you'll want a 4G connection. If you have weak signal, the 'Go Live' button will be grayed out.

Once you've loaded the app, you can then head to your page, your profile or a group. It's still not obviously apparent where you go to stream though! That's because it's hidden away and to find it you need to click on the status/post box as though you were going to write a status.

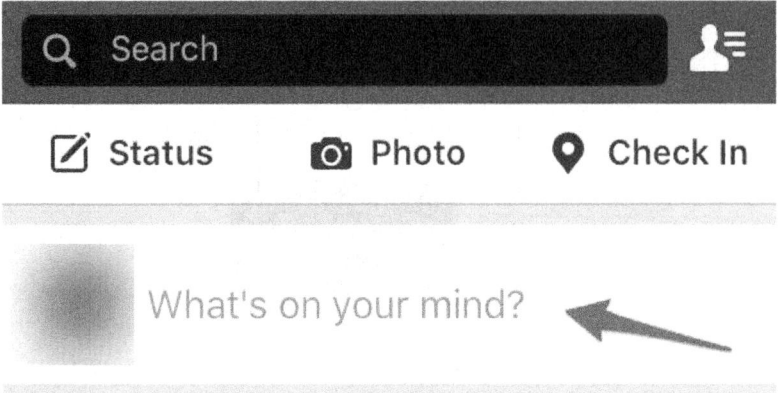

Once you click this, you'll then be greeted with options down the bottom and one of these is the option to livestream. This looks like a small silhouetted figure with radio waves emitting from their head.

Cancel   **Update status**   Post

🔒 Only Me ▾

What's on your mind?

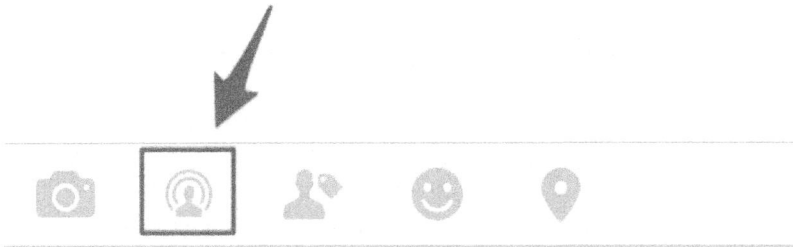

Click this and you'll then be taken to another screen. Here, you'll see your front facing camera alongside the option to create a title and the word 'connecting'.

After a couple of seconds, the 'connecting' sign will turn into a blue button that says 'Go Live'. As you might imagine, you simply have to click this button in order to begin live streaming to your audience.

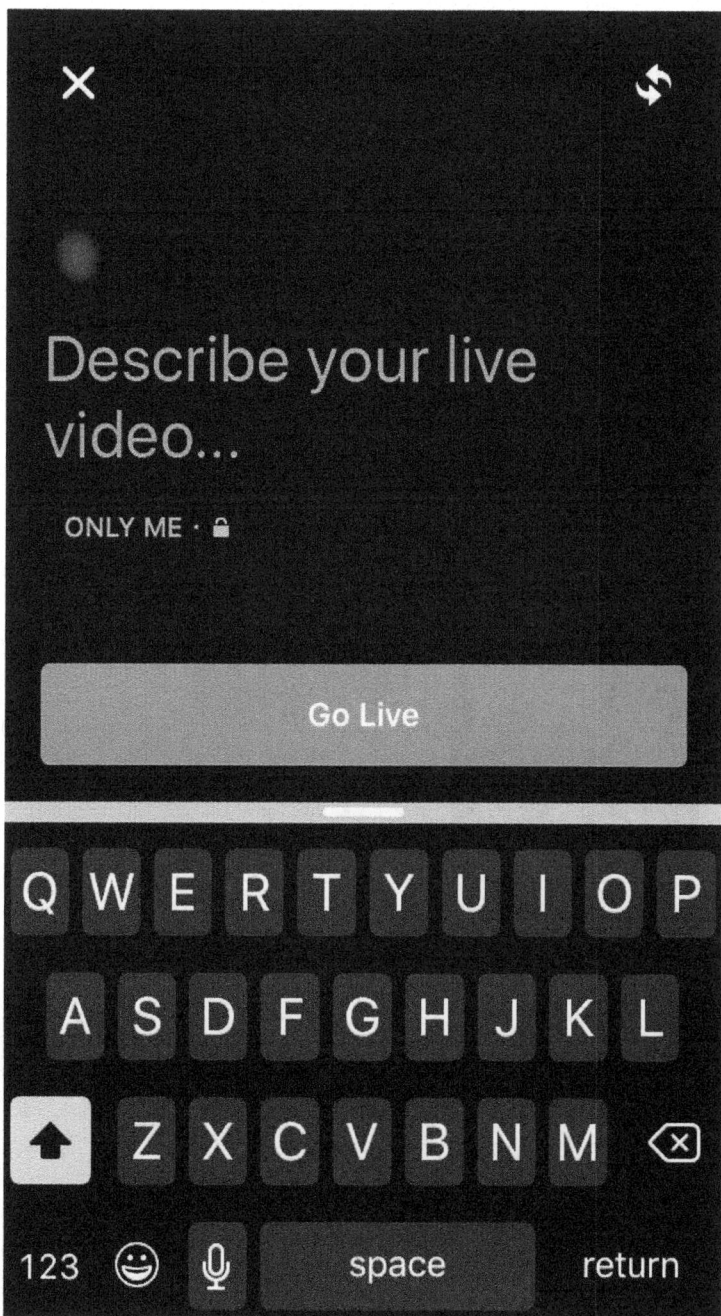

Describe your live video...

ONLY ME · 🔒

Go Live

Q W E R T Y U I O P
A S D F G H J K L
Z X C V B N M ⌫

123 🙂 🎤 space return

Describing the live video is of course important. This is what will allow people to know what you're posting about and whether or not they're interesting in watching.

3. Write a catchy description before going live.

A great description will capture people's attention and help them understand what your broadcast is about.

At the same time, you can also see who you're sharing with. If you hit the button on your own personal profile page, then it will say 'Friends' underneath. Tap that and you can decide to share your live feed publicly, or you can choose to share it in a range of other ways:

- Your home town
- Your current area
- Your close friends
- Your family
- Just yourself
- Friends 'except'

This is a great way to experiment with your own live streaming: you can try creating a video and sharing it with just yourself. This will then allow you to see what the videos look like and to test using the set-up without embarrassing yourself with a low quality video that will be seen by everyone you know/everyone following you!

Note that you can also change where you are posting and who you are posting as. You'll see your own profile in the top left but if you decide to post from your business page instead, then you'll see that instead of your private profile. For instance, if you have a business called 'CatFoodForever' and you post from that page, then you'll see that you're posting as 'CatFoodForever' and it will automatically be public, meaning that everyone will be able to see it. You can't change this option.

Finally, if you post in a group, then only members of that group will be able to see the stream. This is a great feature if you're planning a stag party for example. It means that you can upload videos of the venue you're going to be checking out, or you can even stream events as they happen only people 'in the know' will be able to see.

Note that one more option is to switch between the front-facing and rear-camera on your device. This is useful for flicking between your own commentary and things that you want other people to see.

This is the basic way that you will use Facebook Live to create live streams. There's actually a lot more to learn and use though, so over the next couple of chapters we'll be looking at the more advanced features and how those compare with the features available through other platforms like Periscope.

What Marketers Need to Know

The last section looked at how to create a Facebook Live video generally. As a marketer though, you are looking to create a very specific type of video with a very specific type of objective.

Basically, you're going to want to create your video from your page. Most businesses, blogs and brands should be using a Facebook Page to promote themselves rather than using a profile. To start streaming from here, you then simply have to tap the 'Post' button, then tap anywhere in the text field and then choose the live-stream option.

This will automatically be a public video meaning that anyone can see it if they visit your page and meaning that your viewers can share your videos with other friends.

But for the most part, only people who are following your page will see the content you're creating unless they know someone who is a fan. This means that the best way to build your audience is to build more followers for your page.

The good news though is that live streams you create are more likely to be seen by your followers than other types of content. That's because Facebook is really pushing this type of content and therefore, they want it to be successful! While it's not clear how many of your followers will automatically see your footage, it's certainly true that this is an effective way to get in touch with your followers.

What's also handy is that your followers can choose to subscribe to your live feeds and this way, they'll be notified the next time you go live!

As you broadcast, you'll also be able to see how many people are viewing your content and you'll be able to see any comments or reactions that people leave. They can also post reactions 'emojiis' or 'stickers' in order to show their appreciation, support or vitriol…

Once you've finished recording, you simply tap to stop. At this point, the video will just remain on your Facebook Page for people to continue watching, commenting and 'liking'. This means that you get all the same benefits you would normally get from posting a live video but only with more exposure at the start.

An added bonus is that people will also have *other* ways of discovering your content. For example, they can use the 'Facebook Live Map' in order to see public streams from all around the world. This creates a fantastic opportunity for you to reach a broader audience and to gain more followers and to get more exposure as a result.

Remember, from a marketing standpoint one of the huge strengths of live streaming is your ability to interact with your audience. So make sure you are doing this: respond to the comments you see and say hi to the people who log in!

This is one of the strangest experiences as a viewer. When you log into Facebook Live and watch someone's stream and they say 'Hi John! Thanks for joining me! Do you have any questions?'. This *really* increases engagement and shows the audience just how exciting it is to be present, right there in that moment.

Chapter 3: Advanced Features and Tips

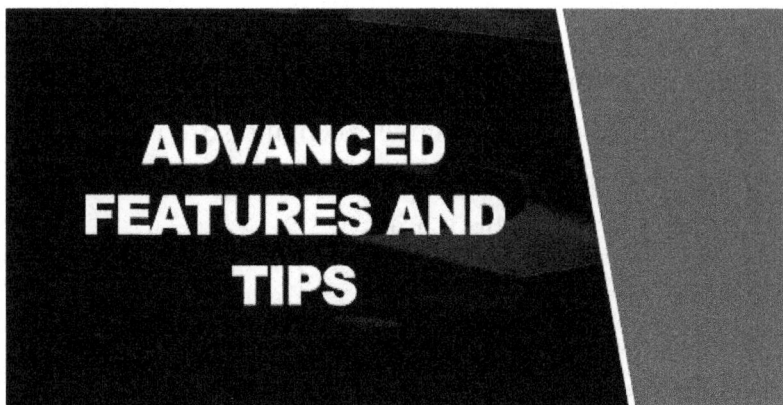

Now you're up and running with Facebook Live, it might be useful to consider some of the other features that the platform offers and some of the other strategies you can use to gain an even bigger audience and succeed on the platform.

In future chapters, we'll look in more detail at how you can make sure the videos themselves are as good as possible.

Editing Video

One very exciting thing that you can do with Facebook Live is to edit your videos once you've posted them. This is a huge benefit as it means that you can make something professional out of your live stream! It's a feature that doesn't exist with the other live streaming tools out there and it's probably one of the very *best* features that sets Facebook Live apart as the best option for now.

Doing this is just the same as editing any other video that you may have posted to Facebook. All you need to do is to click on the date of the post in the timeline to access it and then choose 'edit'.

You'll then be taken to the 'Edit Video' page, where you'll have Basic, Captions and Advanced tabs. Pick 'Basic' and you can choose a category for your video. This will make your video easier to find. You can also create a title and upload a thumbnail. Creating great thumbnails is a very important strategy for getting more people to watch your videos. Facebook, like YouTube, will automatically generate thumbnails based on the content of the video – but you can also pick thumbnails from your existing photos, or upload photos to use yourself.

Another thing you can do is to add a call to action. This is very handy for marketers as it will let you convert directly from your live video! This will normally take the form of a 'Buy Now!' or 'Subscribe Now!' and will require you to choose a URL. Make sure that you include this message verbally in your video too, that way you can direct more sales to your site and the video will be reinforcing what you're saying.

The complete list of options here are:

- No button
- Book now
- Download
- Learn more
- Shop now
- Sign up
- Watch more

There are also more advanced features here too. If you head to 'Captions' for instance, then you can select to upload an SRT File and that way to add captions. Another option is to select Advanced. Here you can find options relating to distribution, which allows you to prohibit embedding. If you tick this button (it is unticked by default) then your fans won't be able to add the video to their own pages. Of course as a marketer, your objective is to get your video seen by as many people as possible. That means you *want* people to share your content and you want them to be able to embed the videos. In short then, leave this one unticked!

Also like other videos on your page, you'll be able to view comments and views that occur after you have uploaded the video to get the total number of likes and of shares.

Viewing the Live Map

One of the very best ways to really understand Facebook Live and to get started with it is to start watching other people's content. And as soon as you start watching a video and someone welcomes you by name, you'll no doubt understand the surreal, voyeuristic nature of Facebook Live.

To use the map, simply navigate to
http://www.Facebook.com/livemap.

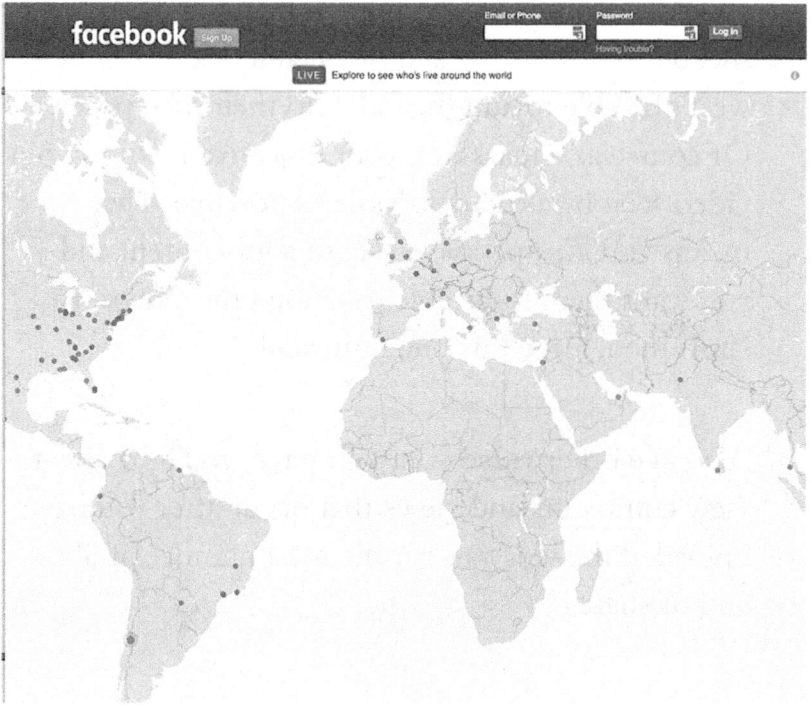

This is a feature that has been borrowed from
Periscope which is a good move, seeing as it is one
of the most popular features and something that is
sorely lacking from Meerkat.

What you'll see when you visit this page, is a simple
grey map with blue pins that show where streams are

coming from. You'll notice that there are cluster in some areas.

You can then move the cursor to move the position of the map and if you hover over a blue pin, you'll be able to get a preview of the video that shows you how many people are watching, the thumbnail and the description. From there, you can then decide if you want to watch or not.

Before you go live yourself, I highly recommend that you take a look at this map and watch some of the content created by other users. This is a great way to see how it works from the point of view of the viewers and it's a great way to get ideas of what to do… and what not to do!

When you look around here, you'll notice a large gulf in terms of the quality of the content. Some videos are live streams from sporting events or television shows. Others are clearly created by experienced YouTubers and marketers who know how to hold an audience. Some are streams of driving or of extreme sports.

Others though are unprofessional rants and will often have zero views. Learn what works and what doesn't and ask yourself what you would want to see more of!

Note that on the map, you can actually see where some viewers are coming from. This is indicated by lines drawn from one part of the world to another. So if a *lot* of people in the UK are watching a video in the US, then a thin line will be drawn that travels from the UK to that pin in the US. You'll also notice that some pins are larger and some even seem to flash.

These are indicators that a pin has a particularly large number of views and it lets you quickly identify the most popular streams without having to hover your mouse over every single one to track down content that is worth watching! Of course 'most popular' and 'worth watching' aren't always the same thing but they do very often go hand in hand it would seem.

To watch a video, simply click on it. From here, you can then comment on the video just like you would comment on any other video, or you can 'react' in the same way you normally would do (long clicking or hovering over the like button to see your options).

Once a stream ends, it will show the words 'This live video has ended' and it will inform you that you'll be able to watch it soon on that user's timeline.

Chapter 4: Facebook Live vs Periscope vs Meerkat

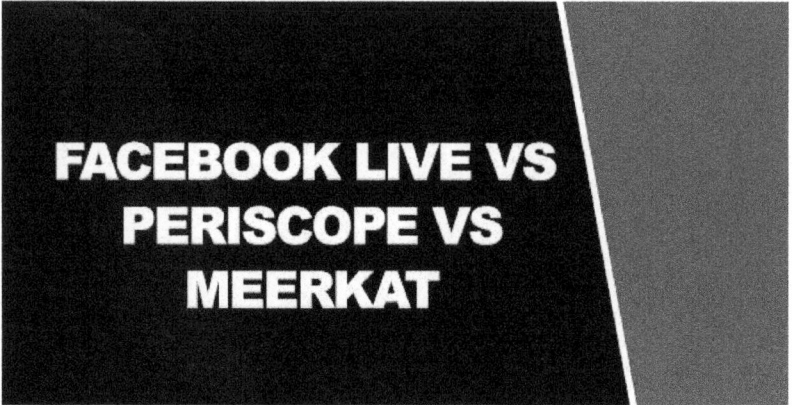

At this point, you should hopefully be convinced as far as live streaming goes. The numbers, the media reaction and the sheer *potential* should be enough to convince you that this is very much the future of online content and certainly the future of video online.

That's not to say that there is no place for pre-recorded video anymore! It merely means that you should be involved in this if you're a marketer and if you want to make the most of the new, exciting opportunity.

But the question still remains: should you choose Facebook over the other live streaming options? Is Facebook Live the one to bet on if you're keen to invest time and effort into live streaming?

The Advantages of Facebook Live

I'm willing to go out on a limb here and say unequivocally: yes. Facebook Live is certainly the best choice for live streaming.

Facebook Live has the very best features and options when it comes to creating exciting live content and sharing it. The fact that you can save all of your content permanently is alone enough reason to get involved, as is the fact that you can promote that content and that you can share it with your existing page followers.

But what *really* makes the huge difference and gives Facebook its massive advantage over the competition is the huge amount of engagement the platform already sees and the fact that you can reach a gigantic audience without having to convince them to get involved.

Jane Goodall
SCIENCE & TECH

Adam Grant, Amy Cuddy + Susan Cain
EDUCATION

Bart Baker
FUNNY

Martha Stewart
FOOD

Denver Broncos
SPORTS

Clemson Football
SPORTS

While you and I now know that live video is quite possibly the future of Facebook and of the web in general, this *isn't* something that your grandma knows – or that many of your friends probably know! While it might sound like there are a lot of users on Periscope, this pales in comparison to the number of users on Facebook, Twitter or Instagram. What's more is that those users are actually trailing off in many ways!

So if you really want to get people to watch your content on those platforms, you're going to have to first convince them to sign up for those platforms in the first place! That means you'll need to message your audience through another channel – perhaps a mailing list or maybe even Facebook – then convince them to create a Periscope profile/download the app and then convince them to tune in when you're live!

Conversely, to start making content on Facebook that will get seen by huge numbers of people, all you have to do is to start filming. Right away your videos will appear on their home feeds without them having to do anything and without them even needing to understand what 'Facebook Live' is. As soon as they start watching though, you can say 'hello' and shock them into new levels of engagement! The difference is subtle but huge and it makes a massive impact on your viewers and on your conversion rates.

At the start of the year, everyone was highly excited for Periscope and Meerkat and speculation was rife as to which would 'win'. Apple names Periscope the best iOS app of 2015. Then Facebook came on the scene a few months later and changed *everything*.

And one commenter summed up what all this means perfectly. Vincenzo M. Landino, CMO, Fifty 2 Creative and host of the Brand Boost Podcast said:

"Facebook Live will completely change the mainstream perception of live streaming upon release to all accounts and blow away all the other options in the market.

"Facebook picking up live streaming for the masses gives credence to the live stream movement. What marketers fail to recognize is that the majority of social media users are not up to date on the latest apps, and many want to use one app for all the features. Facebook is taking that position."

(Note that Facebook actually began letting people use Facebook Live much earlier than December but at first the tool was exclusive to well-known figures.)

Features and Specs

In terms of features, Facebook also manages to keep up with Periscope and Meerkat on almost every facet and in many cases surge ahead.

In terms of the number of users, Facebook is by far ahead. After Facebook is Periscope which has the lead over Meerkat, while another option called 'Blab' is just behind (though it's still in beta).

In terms of the interface, Periscope's is very similar to Facebook. When you log in, you are presented with a map first of all and this is very slick and well put together. You can then see where the periscopes are coming from and choose which ones you want to watch. You can also see a list of current videos. The design of Periscope is crisp, clean and mainly blue. Again, it looks somewhat similar to Facebook.

Meerkat's UI and layout on the other hand is considerably less impressive and even feels a little amateurish. Meerkat uses a very yellow color scheme that some will find a little garish and the only view available is really just a list of different videos and the option to search. It's far less intuitive finding new things and it may be deemed a little crowded and cluttered.

After you have finished recording, Periscope will store your videos for 24 hours allowing other people to watch – after that though it will be lost. Meerkat never saves your videos at all though, meaning that they'll be gone as soon as they're finished. Finally, Blab actually lets you keep your videos forever. We'll see in a moment though that Blab is very different and not really comparable to the other platforms.

For that reason then, Facebook is really your only option if you want to keep the video you worked hard to create. This is another *massive* advantage and another big reason that Persicope and Meerkat may be at risk of becoming obsolete – and so soon after thy crashed onto the market!

One cool feature that Meerkat *does* have in its favour though is the option to use images within your videos. Another handy advantage that both these tools have is the ability to 'schedule' a video. On Facebook right now, you can only post about your forthcoming stream. Other than this though, Facebook pretty much has these platforms beat on every front.

The Odd One Out: 'Blab'

Note that Blab is a little different from the other options here and is in some ways a bit of a hybrid product. While the others are 'one way', Blab is actually more of a conferencing tool that is also live streamed. This allows you to broadcast a video and then to invite people into the 'hot seat' to discuss with you. You can then have up to four people streaming at once, all discussing a certain topic – and the person in that hot seat can change.

While only one person 'hosts' the stream, four people can take part then – and followers of all four participants can see the videos in their feeds. This makes Blab an incredible tool for influencer marketing – you could do an AMA and everyone who sits in the hot seat would promote you to their audience. Likewise, you could watch a video from Tim Ferriss and perhaps be given the chance to feature in the video with him and to be seen by everyone who is a fan of him. Blab also has interesting application as a tool for dealing with social anxiety, as it provides a safe environment to engage in live discussion with strangers! And for marketers, it lets you actually speak *directly* with your visitors.

While Periscope and Meerkat need to quickly up their game, Blab is interesting and unique and might still be useful as an additional area to invest some time in.

Chapter 5: Ideas for Content

So now you know the history of live streaming, you know how Facebook got started with live streaming and you know how to get started. Hopefully you're starting to see the full potential of this new medium and perhaps your mind is beginning to brim with ideas for exciting content you can create.

To help you a little further though, let's take a look at some more types of content that do really well...

Sharing Exciting Moments

If you are building a personal brand, then you might be trying to create an image for yourself. In all likelihood, that image will be of someone who has a great life and who is constantly doing exciting, interesting or unique things. This way, your followers can come to view you as someone who has gotten their life together and if they want to lead a similar life, then they will be all the more likely to listen to your advice and to read your information!

Meanwhile, you want your audience to feel engaged and you want to build trust so that they will read your content and so that they will believe what you have to say.

For all these reasons, simply sharing exciting moments is a great option – and this will also help you to stand out and to reach people who perhaps are not already engaged with your brand.

For example, I was recently trekking through the Swiss Alps with a friend. I have a personal brand that is all about being a digital nomad and living a free lifestyle of travel and adventure by working online. This then made this the perfect thing to share on my channel. I held the camera out at the summit of the mountain and just shared with my audience how still and quiet it was at the top of the mountain. This kind of thing is exciting for you too – sharing that moment with fans makes you feel like you're living the adventure with them!

Likewise, you might opt to stream a concert that you're at, or another live event. Or perhaps you might stream yourself arriving at a new hotel, or at a party or festival. Share your most exciting moments!

Vlogging

But if YouTube has taught us anything, it's that the content you share doesn't have to be exciting at all! Vloggers on YouTube make videos of themselves talking and presenting to their audience and very often this includes nothing but just an insight into their daily lives.

There are many popular vloggers on YouTube for instance who do nothing but provide narration while going about their daily business. Others just talk to the camera. This is the *perfect* kind of content for a personal brand as it allows you to engage even more with your audience and that level of connection and of trust will make all the difference when it comes to getting more sales, followers and subscriptions.

Another tip is to use vlogging that is in-keeping with your niche/industry. One of the most popular options for example is to stream videos of workouts. This is perfect for anyone who is trying to run a fitness blog or sell fitness products.

More Great Formats for Streams

Here are some more great formats for streams:

Top Tips

One thing to remember when creating your content is that you need to cater to people who are just arriving as well as people who have been watching right from the beginning. *Most* of your viewers probably *won't* watch from the start.

This makes structuring your video as 'top tips' perfect – because people can understand each tip without needing the context of the last tip. What's more is that this format is perfect for speaking freely while still having some structure. The list will keep bringing you back to the main topic but you'll be able to speak freely on each point.

Reviews

Live video is ideal for reviews. Again this gives you a good focus while still allowing you to talk freely. At the same time, a review works well live because your viewers can ask questions and ask to see specific things or have you demo specific features. What works *especially* well of course is to review your own products! At this point, it becomes a little like shopping through the TV!

AMAs

An AMA is an 'Ask Me Anything'. This idea was popularized by Reddit and is almost a form of live media in its own right in that format. It's also ideal for discussing things directly with your audience.

Interviews

Why not just conduct an interview? This means your viewers can engage with two people at once and at the same time it means that they can add their own questions.

Discussion

Another option to do some influencer marketing. Get someone well known in your niche around and discuss the subject with them for all to watch. Your viewers can join in.

Tours

A tour of your home, your office or even your local town is a great way to be personal and open with your audience as well as to build your image!

Chapter 6: How to Create Engaging Live Videos

There are some aspects of Facebook Live that are unique from any other form of content. In some ways, what you create for Facebook Live needs to be different from the videos you would create for YouTube. This content has unique challenges – such as dealing with the fact that many people won't watch from the start – and it has unique benefits, like the ability to interact with your viewers.

But at the same time, other aspects are just the same. Some of the tips for creating great live videos are precisely the same as the tips for creating great videos generally. Let's take a look at both…

How to Create Professional Videos

When you create videos with Facebook Live, you are going to be limited in terms of video quality by the camera on your phone. Make sure that you invest in a good quality phone then with a good camera attached. While you might never be able to contend with the quality of production you see on YouTube videos using DSLR cameras, you should still aim to make the experience as crisp and clear for your viewers as possible by investing in a goo camera phone.

But what's in many ways more important is your lighting. If you look at the Facebook Live Map right now, you'll see a lot of videos that look dark, grainy and grimy. This is immediately off-putting for your viewers who won't

64

want to squint through the noise to see your footage.

Making your videos bright can do a huge amount to increase their apparent quality – so either invest in a light box or just make sure you're in a well-lit area by a window. If you do sit near a window, it's usually best to sit at a right angle to it so that half your face is lit. This is called 'Rembrandt lighting' and is one of the most flattering ways to light up your face.

Likewise, make sure that you look good! Unless your aim is to create a very personal feel, you don't want to look like you just rolled out of bed. Wear smart clothes (without trying too hard) and check yourself in a mirror. Think about your 'set' as well and where you want to film. What's behind you? Make sure it's not your washing up!

Just as you can improve the quality of the image without changing the camera, the same goes for your sound quality. Get a phone with a good microphone but think as well about the acoustics of the room you're in and make sure you speak clearly. Avoiding background noise is also always preferable!

Professional Content

When presenting your video, try to speak slowly and clearly and to project your voice as much as you can. Don't shout but certainly don't mumble either!

You want to try and create an intimate and personal feeling for these videos but that doesn't mean you can just ramble on with no planning. The best videos will have some kind of focus and some kind of purpose – so try to use the content tips above to structure your video in a way that lets you keep coming back to the point and that avoids any massive tangents.

Let your audience interact with you and be sure to acknowledge them when they log in or when they comment. And remember that you need to cater to people who are just arriving – keep recapping on what has been said and remember that not everyone has been watching since the start!

Chapter 7: How to Build Your Following and Get More Viewers!

The best way to increase your following for Facebook Live is simple: increase your following on Facebook in general! If you can grow your audience on Facebook, then everything you share will automatically be seen by a larger audience. You can of course also promote your live videos independently but most of your growth will come from tried and true Facebook marketing techniques.

Fortunately, there is no shortage of these techniques!

Facebook Marketing Done Right

The best way to market on Facebook is the same as it is for nearly every other kind of platform online and off – that is to provide *value*.

The aim is to get as many people as possible to want to read your content and to want to share it, like it and comment on it. To do that, you need to create a page that provides a service. The mistake that too many marketers and brands make is to use their Facebook page simply as a place to announce their products and to try and encourage people to buy. They use this simply as a platform to post things like 'Why not buy today and be blown away??' and then they wonder why no one wants to sign up!

The answer? This is essentially spam!

Instead then, look at how you can create something that people will actually want to read. Ask yourself: would *you* want to follow your own page with it the way it is currently? If not, then ask yourself how you could make your posts more interesting and more useful.

Some top strategies include:

- Sharing content that you find through tools like Buzz Sumo where you can see the type of content that is performing particularly well

- Sharing content that you create – and making sure that it offers something unique and that it offers genuine value

- Engaging with your users and responding to questions etc.

- Promoting special offers that provide genuine value to your followers and that help them save money

If you do all this, then you should reach the point where your social media is *in itself* almost a form of service. Ideally people should be very upset if your Facebook page ever went down!

And a top tip: remember that people use Facebook as a means of communication. The most successful content in terms of shares is often the content that people can use to express something about themselves, or that they can use to begin a discussion or show someone they're thinking of them.

Other ways to get even more likes for your page include synchronizing it with your blog (by adding a plugin to provide a live feed for example, or using Facebook comments) and with your other social media accounts. You can also simply place buttons on your site and on your other content that people can click in order to visit your Facebook page and perhaps Like it.

Facebook Live can also be used as part of a sales funnel. A sales funnel is basically a sequence that takes someone from being unfamiliar with your brand to trusting you and wanting to buy from you.

So this might mean that you first grab their attention with a blog post that shows off your knowledge and your great writing style. If they see a few of these, they move to stage two – which is signing up for the mailing list to get your 'free report'.

Very often, the next stage is a 'live conference'. But why not use Facebook again? This is once more an event with a date and time that you can use your mailing list to build hype for and get people excited about.

The difference though is that you'll be running this through a platform that's very new, hip and exciting. And what's more is that they'll actually be able to *respond* to you!

And even when you're not building a funnel in this way, creating suspense and getting people excited for an upcoming video is still a good strategy. You can do this from your Facebook page and from other platforms like Twitter. Try to turn this into an event and get people excited for it!

Using Facebook Ads

Posting great content only gets you so far though. If you really want to make an impact, then you should also consider creating adverts and using these in order to generate more likes for your page which will lead to more views for your live videos.

Facebook Ads are great because they are PPC – or 'Pay Per Click'. This means that as an advertiser, you will only pay when someone actually clicks on one of your adverts and sees your page. That in turn means that if an advert is unsuccessful in that it doesn't generate any clicks, you won't actually have to pay anything for it at all!

But you can actually go one step further than that too – by using CPA. CPA stands for 'Cost Per Action' and this now means that you'll only pay when someone actually takes action. In this case, you can set up a CPA so that you will only pay when someone actually likes your page and therefore you are able to show them your live videos as and when you need to.

Another great feature of Facebook ads is that you can target the people who see them very specifically. This way you can opt to show your ads only to the right type of person who is likely to enjoy your video and who is likely to b interested in buying your products. You can use this then to target people based on their:

- Age
- Sex
- Location
- Interests
- Job description
- Marital status

And more!

Chapter 8: How to Monetize Facebook Live

The key to making this work for you as a money making method is to simply integrate your marketing closely with your product, your advertising and your live videos themselves.

We've already seen how you can use Facebook Live in order to add a call to action on a video. If you also make that call to action in person – so that you are physically asking people to buy your product – then this can be even more effective. It makes a big difference when you actually ask people to buy something in person.

You can this way be much more persuasive and emphatic and as we discussed, you can also answer questions that your potential buyers might have live. This way you can really encourage people to buy something where a sales page or another technique may not have been effective.

Buy then following that plea immediately with a link where they can click to buy your product, you can create a large conversion rate from your Facebook videos.

Try not to make all of your videos sales pitches however! Remember what we already discussed: the key to success in Facebook marketing and the key to getting shares and Likes is to make sure that your videos are usually providing value.

If 9/10 of your videos provide tips or discussion in your niche, or promote your lifestyle and build trust, then you will make that 10th video *much* more effective at selling. Think about the long term plan and don't just try and shift as many units as possible in every single video!

The key then is to work out how much you are earning from your videos and how much you are earning from each follower on your page. This will then allow you to calculate the budget that you can spend on your ads in order to make sure your business is still profitable.

A Simple Sample Business Model

A simple example of how this might work, is if you run a wedding dress shop. In this case, you could create a social media presence on Facebook, Instagram and Twitter where you would show off photos of your most beautiful dresses and really get people to invest in the lifestyle you're promoting and to enjoy and share the photos and the tips.

As you build your loyal following, you can then promote to them using Facebook CPA ads to get more likes and more engagement. But because your *customer* is a very specific type of person, you should use targeted ads that will only be seen by *women* who are *engaged* and who are in a certain age bracket. These women will almost certainly be in the market for dresses, making them the perfect candidates for advertising to.

And then you can upload your live videos. These might be interviews, Q&As or reviews/showcases of certain dresses. More of your followers will be able to see the videos because of the algorithm giving them preferential treatment and you'll be able to answer questions and take direction from your audience, building more trust. Finish with a call to action and then add the CTA button saying 'shop now'!

Chapter 9: Top Tips for Facebook Live Success

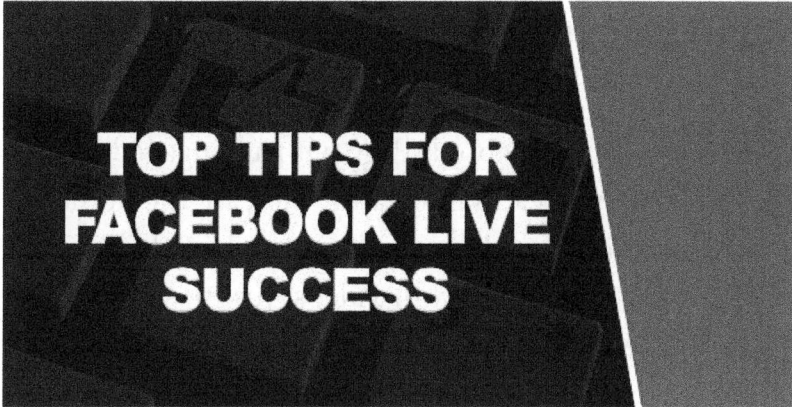

In previous chapters we have looked at tips regarding the type of content to create and how to ensure your footage looks professional. As well though, note that Facebook has its own best practices and tips that it has shared with content creators to try and encourage the highest quality of videos possible.

You can find these here:
https://www.Facebook.com/Facebookmedia/best-practices/live

To recap though, some of the things they recommend include:

Tell people when you're going to broadcast

If you have a Facebook Page with an engaged user base, then you can significantly increase the number of views you'll get by preparing people and telling them to look out for your videos. Just post and say 'Going live at 2pm PST!' or whatever the time is. Likewise, you can also make these posts stand out even more by using hashtags or even tagging individuals!

Wait for a strong connection

If you have a weak connection then your stream will constantly be interrupted by buffering and it might even disconnect. This can result in a very bad experience for your viewers and that might be enough to prevent them from wanting to tune in in future. To avoid letting this happen, make sure that you have a strong signal first. Facebook recommends waiting for either a WiFi signal, or a

4G one. If your connection is too weak to even get started, then the 'Go Live' button will stay greyed out and you won't be able to post.

Write a compelling description

This is very important. And in fact, Facebook recommends that you also have a strong 'point' or topic for your video before you go live. This will help people to know whether or not they might be interested in your video and decide to watch. You don't want people to opt out of watching because the video just looks random – but nor do you want people to watch your videos and then find that they're not interested in what you're saying.

Remember though, this is a 'description' and not just a title. That means you can also sell your video a little. And why not focus on the exciting nature of live streaming too? The example that Facebook does this very well:

We got some great news on jobs and the economy this morning, and President Obama wants to tell you all about it. So pull up a chair in the Roosevelt Room next to his economic team and listen in!

This sounds like you have some kind of privileged access and almost as though you've been invited by the president himself! Just think how much more engaging and exciting that is for an audience.

Invite users to follow

Remember that some people who find your video won't already be following you. Your audience might include people who found you on the live map, or they might include people who saw your post because a friend liked it. So invite them to follow and you can build a bigger audience.

Say hello

We already covered this briefly but remember to respond to comments and to say hi to people as they sign in to watch you. This makes them feel much more engaged and as though they're right there with you!

Experiment with length

Facebook says to broadcast for longer as it will allow you to reach more people. Their recommendation is to go live for at least 10 minutes and the maximum you can stay live for is 90 minutes.

However, it's important to note that there are benefits to shorter content too and this might work better for certain types of content than others. Try different lengths out and see what gets the best response – this is the best way to optimize for your content and your audience!

Go live often and experiment

Another tip from Facebook is to go live often and to experiment with different types of content. We have already been discussing the amazing different types of content you can create and what works well with Facebook Live. But just remember that this is very much a new, exciting and untapped medium. That means that there is still lots of room for experimentation and trying new things.

On their page, Facebook demo some of the more creative videos out there. Comedian Ricky Gervais has a video that he called 'I'm in the bath' which is simply him in the bath, pointing out that he's... in the bath. Meanwhile, Lindsey Vonn is also featured with a video of skiing in New Zealand. The phone is somehow attached so you can 'go with her'.

Posting often meanwhile will also help you to build a bigger audience. Remember as well that one challenge with live video will be the different time zones. Your aim is to reach as many people as possible and to that end, it can be very useful to post regularly so that you can be found by people who might have missed you earlier on.

Note as well that people will watch all *kinds* of content on Facebook Live. People are naturally very voyeuristic and they love being able to get a glimpse into your life. This is especially true if you have a personal brand that you have built up and if you have a lot of real 'fans' who love the content you produce and want to get as close to you as possible.

In other words: don't presume that people won't want to see a certain type of content. If you are doing something interesting or exciting, then consider posting about it so that they can see it! As mentioned, Ricky Gervais posted just because he was in the bath! Don't worry too much if your post is 'off message' – experiment, play around and see what works for you!

Chapter 10: The Future of Live Streaming

Live Streaming isn't Facebook's only interest right now though. The company is looking into a number of very exciting technologies and what's *truly* exciting is the way that all this research and all this technology might come together in the future. Facebook appears to be attempting to corner commercial communication across the web in its entirety and is also investing a fair amount into R&D and future technologies.

For instance, Facebook bought its rival Instagram for a whopping $1,000,000,000. This is a tool that users can use to upload photos and apply effects. It's an artistic form of self-expression and now deeply integrated with Facebook. WhatsApp meanwhile is a live messaging service that could arguably have been seen as a rival for Facebook's own messaging service… until it purchased the company for $19 billion.

In some ways you could consider WhatsApp to bridge a gap between Facebook and conventional messaging, as people will often share photos and videos with groups of people live while events are taking place.

Perhaps one of the highest profile acquisitions of all though was Oculus VR. This is a virtual reality company owned by CEO and founder Palmer Luckey. Through Kickstarter, Oculus managed to create the world's first major contender in the VR space: The Oculus Rift. Facebook bought Oculus VR for an incredible $2,000,000,000 and expressed an interest in developing the tool for live communication.

Imagine being able to be on other sides of the Earth but still have a conversation with a friend or colleague as though they were in the room with you

– able to view their gestures, body language and more! That is the future as far as Facebook is concerned.

And imagine how these technologies might coalesce. Imagine using a 360 camera to stream live footage and then imagine using the Oculus Rift to actually *be there* in VR. You could literally share your experiences, to the point where a friend could be sitting at home and looking around the environment you're in: enjoying all the sights and sounds *as* they happen!

The technology isn't quite there yet and mobile data is a limiting factor at the very least. When connections become faster we can expect 360 video to be much more of a reality, viewed through VR and even recorded using drones perhaps! At the very least, we can expect to see 'live' thumbnails, potentially giving us simultaneous live feeds of the same event from hundreds of different angles… The potential for this technology is almost endless…

This is very probably the direction that Mark and Facebook are heading in. And you can see now why live streaming plays such an integral part in the future for the company – and for humanity!

Right now, live streaming is an exciting opportunity for marketers and an interesting diversion for the general public. But if you bet on it early on, you might just be in a position to take full advantage of the platform when it inevitably becomes a crucial part of the way we communicate.

To finish this section, let's take a look at some of the quotes Mark has shared regarding his interests in developing the company going forward. These shine a very interesting light on the company and its future direction:

"We're working on VR because I think it's the next major computing and communication platform after phones. In the future we'll probably still carry phones in our pockets, but I think we'll also have glasses on our faces that can help us out throughout the day and give us the ability to share our experiences with those we love in completely immersive and new ways that aren't possible today.

"Second, we're working on AI because we think more intelligent services will be much more useful for you to use. For

example, if we had computers that could understand the meaning of the posts in News Feed and show you more things you're interested in, that would be pretty amazing. Similarly, if we could build computers that could understand what's in an image and could tell a blind person who otherwise couldn't see that image, that would be pretty amazing as well. This is all within our reach and I hope we can deliver it in the next 10 years.

"We're working on spreading internet access around the world through Internet.org. This is the most basic tool people need to get the benefits of the internet — jobs, education, communication, etc. Today, almost 2/3 of the world has no internet access. In the next 10 years, Internet.org has the potential to help connect hundreds of millions or billions of people who do not have access to the internet today.

"As a side point, research has found that for every 10 people who gain access to the internet, about 1 person is raised out of poverty. So if we can connect the 4 billion people in the world who are unconnected, we can potentially raise 400 million people out of poverty. That's perhaps one of the greatest things we can do in the world."

Conclusion & Summary

So there you have it: that's pretty much everything you could possibly need to know about Facebook Live. Hopefully you now have a good understanding of just how important live streaming is for the future of the web and what a big role Facebook is likely to play in all this. Mark Zuckerberg himself believes that this might someday be the primary form of content on Facebook – and that has got to count for something!

And in the meantime, live streaming is a completely open market. There is so little competition here that almost every time you go live, you are likely to come away with new followers and subscribers! This is your opportunity to get ahead of the competition and to build a huge audience before others cotton on.

So get involved and start creating live content! You may just find that it's surprisingly good fun once you get involved!

Here are some takeaways to keep in mind while you go about it:

- Facebook Live is the platform with the best chance of conquering live streaming

- But Blab is a useful place to check out too for influencer marketing!

- Lots of things work in live streaming – people love to feel voyeuristic!

- Try to experiment with different kinds of content

- Cater for the people who have watched from the start and the people who are just tuning in

- Think about the best structure for your content

- Use CPA and ads to promote your page

- Always focus on providing quality!

- Ask people to subscribe

- Invest in a good camera phone!

- Acknowledge your viewers by name

- Watch others to see what they do

Appendix: Facebook Live Checklist

Checklist

Looking to make a splash on Facebook Live? This checklist will make sure you have all the crucial details in one place and will walk you through all the steps. This cheat sheet distils all the information found in *Facebook Live Authority* in a format that is easy to follow and easy to pin to your notice board!

The Importance of Facebook Live

Let's start with the importance of Facebook Live. Here are some stats that will remind you why you're doing this and why it's such a big deal...

- Facebook today has over 1 billion users logging in *daily*
- There are more than 1.39 billion users on Facebook Mobile alone
- There are over 300 million photographs on Facebook
- And the average American spends 40 minutes on the site
- Facebook's algorithms have been tweaked to 'favor' live video. This content is more likely to show at the top of a home feed than a photo or a regular video.
- Periscope has well over 10,000,0000 user accounts
- And over 40 years' worth of footage
- Periscope got tweeted about over 60k times when it launched
- Periscope was bought by Twitter for $100 million
- 2 million users on Periscope are active every single day

- Blab users spend over 65 minutes a day watching videos on average
- In 2015, YouTube live-streamed E3 and had over 8 million views in 12 hours
- In six months, Facebook Live had over 246,000 live streams
- Together, these videos garnered over 5.7 billion views
- Mark Zuckerberg is reported saying he is 'obsessed' with Live Video!

How to Create Live Video

So how do you create live video on Facebook as a marketer? It's actually extraordinarily simple. Just:

1. Log in to Facebook
2. Head over to your Facebook page
3. Click to post something new
4. Tap the live stream icon
5. Write a description
6. Hit 'go live'

7. You can tap the icon in the top right in order to switch between the front and rear camera
8. You can see new viewers logging in and respond to comments and likes

There are some other ways you can use Facebook Live as well.

For example:

☐ Post to your personal profile and you can choose who gets to see your feed
   o Anyone
   o Just your contacts
   o Just your close friends/friends from a particular group
   o Just you

☐ Post to a private group so that only those who are in the group see the video

Advanced Facebook Live Features

There are also some more 'advanced' features to consider:

- ☐ Visit the 'Facebook Live Map' in order to see content that other users have created. This can be a great place to get inspiration.
- ☐ Add a 'call to action' button at the end of your video. This will work particularly well if you also verbally include a call-to-action at the end of the video.

- ☐ Your videos will stay on your page long after you've created them and you'll then be able to 'edit' them by changing your thumbnail and adding annotations etc.

Best Practices for Creating the Best Content on Facebook Live

While it's really up to you what kind of content you're going to create on Facebook Live, there are some tips that can help your content to perform as well as possible. These include:

☐ Always ensuring you have a good connection
☐ Choosing a great description for your video so that it stands out and sounds interesting
☐ Asking people who are watching to follow you if they're enjoying your content
☐ Welcoming people who tune in
☐ Responding to comments
☐ Using a high quality camera phone and mic
☐ Speaking clearly and slowly

☐ Thinking about lighting and backdrop – don't let the background distract from the content!

☐ Recapping what you're discussing for viewers just tuning in

☐ Think about the acoustics in the room

Types of Content

There are also some particular types of content that perform especially well and are well suited to the platform:

- ☐ Voyeuristic content and vlogging – Let your viewers get to know you by sitting in on your workouts or hearing your thoughts over your morning coffee
- ☐ Events and trips – Let your viewers attend concerts with you or conferences. If you're hiking through the Swiss alps, let your viewers see this too!
- ☐ Reviews
- ☐ Interviews
- ☐ AMAs
- ☐ Seminars
- ☐ Lessons
- ☐ 'Top 10s'

Sales Funnel

A sales funnel takes this one step further by getting people gradually more involved in what you're doing and getting them more and more likely to want to buy.

A sales funnel will ideally include five "touches" -- that is five interactions with your potential audience.

This can take the form of:

☐ Blog

☐ Email newsletters

☐ Free online webinar

☐ Cheap product

☐ Expensive product

Each of these things will promote the next thing on the ladder and each time the user takes a step they become more actively involved and more likely to spend money with you.

Another example is to use a free report which you can deliver by email.

Cheap products are an important step to get people used to the idea of spending money through your payment portal before they're asked to spend something big.

That's the entire blueprint, so now all that's left is to make it happen!

Made in the USA
Las Vegas, NV
17 February 2021